Modes of Persuasion

Erin Badough

NeoPoiesisPress.com

NeoPoiesis Press, LLC

2775 Harbor Ave SW, Suite D, Seattle, WA 98126-2138
Inquiries: Info@NeoPoiesisPress.com
NeoPoiesisPress.com

Copyright © 2015 by Erin Badough

All rights reserved. No part of this book may be used or reproduced in any manner whatsoever without express written permission from the publisher except in the case of brief quotations embodied in critical articles and reviews.

Erin Badough – Modes of Persuasion
ISBN 978-0-9892018-9-6 (paperback : alk. paper)
    1. Poetry. 2. Erotica. I. Badough, Erin. II. Modes of Persuasion.

Library of Congress Control Number: 2015913865

First Edition

Cover Design: Milo Duffin and Stephen Roxborough

Printed in the United States of America.

*for Michelle, Rose, Tamitha,
and especially Dale,
for giving me a voice*

*to all the women without one,
i humbly request the honor*

Contents

ethos

bedouin 7
devouring 8
three minute steep 9
affection 10
enchanted rock 12
inspired connection 14
dead words 26
the whores of Babylon 16
philophobia 18
devoid of 20
balance 22
a wetted languor 24
enshadowed 26
ex-aqua 30
an indeterminate state of being 28
Chandni Chowk 30

logos

survival strategy 35
periodic 36
just another love song 38
waiting for the bus 40
steeping in time, darkly 41
waste little, want much 42
a seed strewn into the garden 44
hesitant under a scalding sky 46
holy water 48
the followers 50
not quite living, not quite dying 51
slow dance (last stand) 54
beach city sunrise 56
humble pie 57
he liked to watch 58
saviour (housekeeper of souls) 60

pathos

Adam's apples	63
the feast of sinners	64
the punishment	65
demolition	70
downward from skinned	72
in violent umbrage	74
vindication	75
Osama	76
candy-colored foes and thoughts of war	80
just a girl, after all	82
child, with child	84
a promise of peace	86
leaves	89
sixlets	90
oil slick	92

eros

ginger crush	95
orchis dracula vampira	96
incurable	98
after b'stilla, before the morning	100
the almond	102
a timorous potency	104
commune with me	106
cocoa flow	107
the whipping post	110
barefoot and amorous	112
of pain and pleasure	113
cherry tomato	114
in medias res	115
melagrana salate	116
goddess	117
vibrations	118
like bees do	119

some like it rough	120
belonging	124
AsFixia	126
extra credit (after school project)	128
d(wh(y))/d(se(x))	130
hush	132
like molasses on a soft summer morning	134
rise now, falling	135
at the end of her rope	136

ethos

bedouin

the root of her name
the nape of her fiber
the undeniable force on her waking hours

she ached
each time the wind wept in a different direction

she dreamt
of foggy mornings and cold rocky outcrops from afar

though sitting still
desperate from lack of direction
she was never stagnant within
moving back and forth
with the pull and tug
of the moon's fleeting fancy

never at peace

unless her feet were wandering on foreign soil
unfamiliar territory
unmapped from her soles to her soul

devouring

time collected in saliva pools   *if I*
under his restless tongue
rubbing the tip
along the length of his lower jaw
in a sweeping arc   *could*
lips parted slightly
to allow the moist air entrance

he swallowed slowly   *cannibalize*
feeling the drool ooze down
the pitted esophageal tunnel
present(ce) giving way to   *my thoughts*
bleak of unrealizable future

he couldn't stomach the acidic burn   *into*
dissolving him doggedly by regurgitation
so he stopped filling the void with food   *bite-sized*

there were no new flavors to fantasize over
anymore   *pieces*

weary
he drank his weight in water
until his cellular thoughts   *I still*
exploded

drowned in a wash of saltless sensation   *wouldn't*

three minute steep

let the letters of my longing
seep into your pores
one note at a time

gather the cupped fluid
just shy of boiling
to your sun-caked lips
hands trembling with trepidation

feel the steam roll
along your cheeks and your nose
kiss lightly upon your eyelids
tumble into your hair

drink daintily from the edge
of the wide brim, the heat burning
the tip of your tongue
in an affectionately painful tingling
that slides down the centerline
of your body

warm to my touch
toes up
and bend slightly at the shoulders
for another simmering sip

content

affectation

you baffle me.

you do not move in a mathematical manner. you walk as if purposely uneven, a shuffle-clap of mismatched limbs struggling to hold dominance over each other. there is nothing dominant in your nature. you give way under the damp pressure of my palms as if afraid of your own strength, afraid to challenge my smaller structure. you need the bile of servitude to remind you of your own humanity.

I do not know if I can hold this farce of force much longer.

I long to be the river reed bending, but not breaking, within your fingertips. you have buried my roots in rain drops, and they seek the rich and moist soil far below. I float in defiance of my desires. I can't get deep enough, can't reach the firmament. the water of your weakness keeps me from settling where I know I belong.

I was born with leaves and lilies instead of legs, unable to remove myself from you.

I crave the calcium coalescing below your flowing bed. instead, I choke on your algal death. the overabundance of phosphorus and nitrogen suffocates me slowly into rot. I know I will end up like the other cypress knees, flotsam discarded from the trunk as an unwanted parasite. my wood will dry and turn brittle until there is no more flexure, snapping from the strength you will gain as I grow more weary. a siphon, you will bleed me dry until my roots weep in obsolescence. you will grow miry with newfound vigor. now stagnant, your once clean water will become thick enough to chew. only then will I sink to the bottom.

my carcass will enrich the bottom of your wells. the decay will lead to new lotus blossoms and bristle of bony tree knobs seeking air. they will float over my remains, dreaming of a rich calcine promise you will never bestow on them.

only when dead do you allow anyone to learn of your true nature.

I cry silent warnings of outrage from my grave, but no one listens.

enchanted rock

as I look
into the face of the calmly sipping lake
I see a water nymph blinking back
amazed at the resemblance

the water so clear
I can almost feel the smooth
petrous promises laying snug
against my palm

I close my eyes
hear the wind and chatter of the leaves
thinking suicidal thoughts from high in the trees
I sink slowly into the ground
feet crossed neatly beneath me

the twigs and flakes of bark
scratch lightly
at my legs, seeking
a rare recognition from a warmer body

today I'm not warm

the autumn air swirls around me
as I shrink beneath the lining of
my jacket
my armor

I wonder why I'm still sitting here

I open my eyes and look down

from this proximity
the mirror has lost its reflection
I am awash in the acrylic glare

of vernal brown
winter grey
sorbing into each other
in a sway of color

the pebbles have disappeared

I focus on the painted peaks

I see again the mirror
of my eyes
my hair
my mouth
dancing on the waves

I lose the sensation of sound

I wonder which is more real

this lively reflection in the water
or this sedate reality on land

I close my eyes again
lean in closer
and hear the brush
sweeping softly across the canvas
a wailing wake trailing behind

the stroke is fast
and the bristles left behind burrow under

pieces of me

inspired connection

I am one in many and many in one

I am the breath
that animates the sun and
shines within the constellations

I am the sound of footsteps
falling on stones and
echoing against the ripples of wind-combed water

I am the verdant hills
that crinkle the earth beneath
ripe, pregnant pastures and groves
pushing up towards the sky in a
random manner of craving

I am the tree that sways, whispers, watches, and waits
but never breaks

I am the worm
that wriggles through the rooted humus
symbiotic in my search for
muddy playgrounds and mineral-rich gifts

I am the passing of time,
one second collapsing on the next in a rush
towards the future and its unknown potential,
seeking new possibilities in favor of old failures

I am the Big Bang
the death of a star, light years away,
the skin of an apple, the seeds of a raspberry

I am chocolate and vanilla
unswirled

I am this moment
in a space shared with you
where there is room for all of the molecules in the universe

in the continually collapsing manner of a black hole

in the ever expanding manner of love

the whores of Babylon

speak sweetly
so softly
we sisters three

snipping your hair
so gently
while you
sleep; prickle your
thumb and boil
your stewing
steep until the
sulfur essence
bubbles free

cast a confusion
'pon your sticky soul

grind up
your gristle
salt into the pot

gyrate chants
circuitous
as a sot

dip budding pelvis slow
into your bowl

excrete sins
and mix in
svelte
lithe
replete

our toes we raise to quivered breast

ready
the pound of slavered drum
beats on
steady
and we gasp

unison

the spell complete

this fantasy
that dances
on your head

lies quietly in dream
'til we are dead

philophobia

she lies
luxuriant
in the comfort of her own skin

reveling in the sensation
of a summer breeze
wafting lightly against her

down

she feels
independent of thought
in this thickly darkened room
sheltered from the scorch of an undying day

she closes her eyes
hears the whirring of the fan
as the blades twirl endlessly
and recalls the touch
of midnight caresses
and endless hands

imagined
but never
possessed

the keys
clinking on the dimpled sheets
at her hardened feet
do not open the lock

as they scratch her heels
she wonders
if she will ever find the right ones

perfectly cut and sized
greased and oiled

ready
and waiting

waiting
like she is

to jump
to dive

to sink to the bottom
and wallow among the riverbed riches

she opens her eyes

the curtains are still there

devoid of

the tick-tock
notes the blurry passage of fog
every saturated moment an echo
of the previous

the hollow die is cast
a solitary snake eye
staring through the empty suggestion of
her barren form
scraping through the day
towards nightly oblivion

once
she thought she saw the sun
but it was merely a low-hung moon
reddened in gluttonous abandon

now
she collects oil-slick feathers
that glisten in the dark
amid the glowing yellow-eye beads
that see through her whispers
into the pitch beyond her pupils

where abstracts are
consumed
saturated
reshaped

into the whimsies and monsters
of her youth; a metaphor for something
unspoken and unnamed

this beating of wings
this screeching of worms

this tunneling of earth
this death
is of the mind
alone

her legs collapse
on the wetted tongue of soil
spilled carelessly against the parched clay

she can feel the scratch of delicate roots
giving way beneath her being

she raises her palms close to her face
to examine the lines of life

there is no truth there

dismayed, she buries these Judas hands
in the scattered blackened humus
praying that Spring will bring
new skin
new colors
new air

she holds her breath
and wilts

balance

I
am
white on white
a stain
atop an oily
stain
homogenous in my
bewilderment
at day and night
breathing
the driving force that bends the knee
catapulting one foot before the other

endless
the world is
endless
and I am at the bottom
trying to dig into the dark
further
a little
further
into the wash
the emptiness
where there is no color
no noise
no expectation or need

but this is the wrong direction
a false truth
where my feet fly into the air
and my head hangs into the sand

the air
between the bits
of shell

will only maintain
a semblance of
life
and in such a
life
I am but a sliver
yearning to be a π

what is the end
where do
I
end
.

a wetted languor

her body laid out
spread among the green grass blades
each cutting a few cells deep
staining her eyelids

like memory

with shadowed lips
she prayed in the pearled glow of a pregnant night

to be pummeled slowly into an earthen bed
that she might sleep in the forever
of silence
of stillness

in the tranquility of this moment
without presence

dark lashes fell over her heavy sight
and she dreamt of rain
rain that fell slowly
yet determined
in wet dollops on her forehead
her cheeks
and combed her hair into silvern slivers

she felt the lazy randomness of sky
falling against her slightly parted mouth
the unrepentant gravitational pull of nature
holding her still and washing away her skin
until shamrocks began to sprout
from beneath her quivering torso

in her mind's eye
she saw a flower grow to bursting

from beneath her navel
coating her in a dusty pollen
bees feasted on the gathering
between her knees
until she was covered in clover
worn away
with the blossom of countless purple flowers

everything smelled of her

some time later
she awoke
stiffened from the rough cushion of soil
beneath

the sun began to peek over that imaginary line
somewhere in the distant future
and in this growth of light
she first noticed her hands
the color of West Texas mud
with a slight kiss of chlorophyll
lingering on her elbows and on the top of on her tongue

the smudge of bitter herbs

crushed
cleansed
new

dead words

I stand on the bones of dead pens
and cry my wrath unto the world
what portion of it deign to listen
with this chalk I write
of my blood
of my landscape
of my horizon that blinks incessantly
beyond metaphorical glass ceilings

I cannot scrawl on the snowy clouds
for the earth is in my bosom
and I hold her most sacred
more than breath itself

life pumps as sap through my wooden veins
and I dream of shedding this autumn coat
and budding anew with spring

in the desperate depths of winter,
when that crushed calcium
is lost on the lascivious winds
I shall carve my embered soul into the rocks with charcoal

enshadowed

the sky is a husky, barren slate
the lone crow is cackling the dying of another day

like a death knell
or a church bell

or maybe both

the wind doesn't whistle
but howls quietly
unsure of why it is blowing

I listen to its wailing
feeling vast

        and blue
           and empty
              and small

compared to the pebbles grumbling perturbedly
underneath my steps
wondering why
I couldn't have picked another path

for them
I have no answer but
continuance

an indeterminate state of being

for her
it is that undecided nature
of the platypus
that indistinct fantasy of oil
trying to sink beneath the water

awash on the heaving waves
she wonders at the idea
of surrender

to drift
        against the sandy bottom

to expand freely

undefined

        to the pillowed depths
        while the significant stature of dissolved salt
        presses against her torso
        until she is finally able to succumb

is there a treasure of trust
in this buried wooden chest

no

it remains empty of all but rust

interim

she is comprised of sediments and chlorides
she the column
and the fist that tumbled it
to the ground

no one can provide clarification

so she stays seated on the surface
muddy
half-in
breathing starlight

the (skeleton) key remains
hidden beneath her ribs

lost of vision
she dwells in sensations

>*the wisp of silk stockings*
>*the caress of softened leather*
>*the potency of latex*

    and salivates

ex-aqua

office chair in a field
watching the dandelions
dreaming of enclosed spaces

Chandni Chowk

suffocating spices sizzle
in the air, more
turmeric and
chili than
oxygen.
black
diesel
smoke
permeates
the senses,
wafting
deftly
through-
out the
market-
place;
bodies
filling
every void
surrounding,
oblivious to the
mounting
chaos.
moving
road blocks
fill the streets,
carts, bicycles,
people sandwiched
in between. amid the ruckus
I stand, an alabaster rock on a black lava
shore, in awe of the orchestrated circus before me,
embarrassed by my mounting trepidation and desperate
desire to be rescued from this overwhelming madness,
this deserted island, to a faraway English oasis
where I can breathe and see for miles.

logos

survival strategy

an oak tree does not judge

it accepts its fate
to root into the ground with great purpose
and reach for the sky in promise of sun

it expands the breadth of its limbs
devouring carbon dioxide and heat
converting that light into growth and rebirth

it does not worry about
the size of its growth rings
whether the soil will provide nutrition
in the coming days

if there is no food available
the tree seeks it out
spreading, invading
until it is fed

sustained

its bark is as thick as need be
its acorns as plentiful as the earth allows

there is no glass ceiling
and concrete is no obstacle to its strength

periodic

the sky is a dingy shade of grey
bringing no promise of rain
leaving Hope sitting on the horizon
blue eyes clogged and polluted

if I were rain drops
I'd sear beyond point of vaporization
before ever plinking against that fissured skin

I'd move drunkenly
in the void of interaction
between positive
neutral
negative colloidals
until collapsing

stick figure graffiti against a blank wall

it's too hot to sit still and liquefy
so I wander from room to room

the world is unstable

in the interim
I am occupied
with partitioning my mind into isomers
staring into the eyes of my poorly made copies
until vision is blurred
epithets slurred
against them that touch the world

in such a skin-flinching reality
how is Einsteinium to compete with Helium

noble gases
merely occupy themselves with their
perfection

there is character in complexity
and you are nothing more
than Hydrogen

just another love song

just another love song
for a girl that will never look lovingly

the bleat bleat of heart notes
falls on deaf ears
dreaming of passion
swelling
that dies in the summer heat
never to be realized

but they don't see their follies

they see the hope
the fawning of young souls
making warmth and promise
where none presides

they see and feel the fulfillment
of an age where they are wise
beyond measure
though smaller in stance
shorter in stamina

these men, they live in hope
for the promise of beauty
planted indeterminately

they see the blossom of cheek
over full bloom of heart

they long for the tightness of skin
in place of a sure-footed stead

there is a calamitous chasm
where they seek and dream
of a crevice of soft clay

malleable in the downpour

true warmth of touch is in the experience
and experimentation
of the wanting woman
that is not afraid to know
what *feeling* really means

whispers in dark corners are no match

subservience isn't the apex of being
it is the nadir of apathy

and you can love like the somnambulist
in another bedroom
this is where the fire is
and the rubbing of your skin
is putting out the flame

waiting for the bus

Little Boy
kicking ant piles
watching them scatter
rise to arms
madcap ruin

Little Girl
watching Little Boy
waiting for the ants
to bite him
in retribution

steeping in time, darkly

dark vermilion promises
gathered around glass windows
a soul source of light
into the shadows of your cellar
crumbling and flaking
from a constant slow chipping
of putrid passive-aggressive clatter
reeking of sulphur
stinking of flesh and abandon

dark lacquered banisters
sliding up the stairway
raising your pale-eyed
sub-consciousness
to the whisper of ghosts
fornicating in secret nooks

creation!

the final yank of the wool, down

dark colored tiles
grasping each other eagerly
in a grout stained puzzle
blankly reminiscent
of dusty beginnings
and calcite endings
laughing silently
in echo
at our pathetic persistent fumbling
towards a
dark desire for immortality

a lie
to escape the truth
of fear

paint can hide a multitude of sins

waste little, want much

Be melting snow.
Wash yourself of yourself.
A white flower grows in the quietness.
Let your tongue become that flower.
			Be Melting Snow, Rumi

there is beauty in the simple transient state
to not be defined by an exactitude
of gas, liquid, or solid
maintain a convective entropy
and randomly gather warmth
love, knowledge, and go
so armed into the chaotic world
never be static, for in living
there is so much to know
be melting snow

do not fool your hands or your eyes
into thinking they discern
what days ought to contain
and what will, in the end, come
one divisive moment at a time
do not set your soul on a shelf
afraid of catching fire
or shattering like glass
nothing soils self like fear itself
wash yourself of yourself

cleansed in the winter hush
through the slush grows great promise
in the tired name of Spring
a steadfast and earthy goddess
she is not a likely thing to give way
under the leather boots of duress
the freezing ground may suffocate her garden

the weaker bulbs surrendering, barren and leafless
but in spite (because) of this bitter distress
a white flower grows in the quietness

it blinks a feathered promise
on a frozen sky
slender stem of fibrous green
connecting the shivering petals
to the nutrient-earth
a nurturing bed, a detrital power
your budding taste too can bloom
in the most glacial hour, if well rooted
each memory, each morsel lustily devoured
let your tongue become that flower

a seed strewn into the garden

Close your mouth against food.
Taste the lover's mouth in yours.
You moan "She left me." "He left me."
Twenty more will come.
               A Community of Spirit, Rumi

you feel as a broken body
strewn about on the hardwood floor
the bones of a soothsayer
what shall we in our ignorance learn
from your footless ladder fall? Shall we see
the white of your teeth deeply grooved
from your continuous habit of gnashing
on cold metal tines of inevitability
such slovenly swallows, mouth open and crude
close your mouth against food

fast in the purity of sour love lost
once the rich red wine
dripped over your tongue
in succulent ribbonned textures
unfolding like a flower
pink paintbrush on the dark outdoors
of another's ruby soul
a commingle of desire to whip and to bleed
stirred into the need to grovel on dirt floors
taste the lover's mouth in yours

no more, for the sweet bloom has withered
it is fall, and you lie, blighted
collapsing in your oversized bed
like the russet leaves from the trees in the yard
the shutters are drawn
sky hovering in bleak grey sympathy
oil collects on your pores
vinegar wallowing low against your glands

and in time with the tides of the sea
you moan "She left me." "He left me."

but slumber does not always lead to rest
you must rise, rebirth that hope with day
as the phoenix, alight from the hottest fire
raise your head to the sun
and stand strong on your wearied feet
this journey can be harder than some
but broken roots give cause to watch your step
till the soil you stand on and dream of spring
for one lover lost is as the pit of a plum
twenty more will come

hesitant under a scalding sky

the sun

it's merciless
in that blinding burning sort of way
that leaves you blistered and flaking
with withering skin
desperate to escape the heat
of baking flesh

and yet

he walks on
one foot in front of the other
never thinking of turning back
he presses on around the curve of cliff
jutting up rockily from the brief shoreline

the beach has been washed away
in the low tide

his feet shuffle forward
aimless

there isn't an ounce of shade in sight

finally the road gives way
to dirt path

he pauses
looks on
the future appearing every bit like
the ground he just traversed

weary bent from the
unrelenting heat
he looks forward

then back

he knows where he came from
There are trees to protect him

so he turns around
retracing blind steps to
where the sand is more plentiful
where he can hide
under arbored awnings

from the sun

holy water

it's been a good day
when your clothes are soaked
your arms feel like rubber
and your legs are leadened
when your body kicks your head in
for being mule enough to try and wander
to think about what you'd rather not

I knew he was right
he had spent every day of his life
out before light and in after dark
wasting no sun on self-pity
for there was always work to be done
my granddad, the leather skinned man

I had no crops or livestock to tend
but I know the price of wisdom when heard

it's pouring rain, cats and dogs
if indeed they ever looked and sounded
like watery rocks crashing on a tin roof
but my mind is trying to dig up old memories
wasting away in this prison cell of a house

I put on my shoes and go outside
I am wet under my skin after just thirty seconds
but I have already forgotten what I didn't want to remember
and I take off running down the street
running through massive puddles collected on sidewalks

block after block
of cracked concrete and packed driveways
I know my feet are already raw and soaked through
but I don't really care anymore
the rain is cleansing

I fall to the ground as I return to my front yard
lying face up, I let the rain drops beat into me
condense and erode everything that tries to prick me
at that vulnerable spot near the base of my skull

I ease myself from the floating grassy arena
my arms are like rubber, my legs leadened
I strip the wet clothes from my body
and stand in my living room by the fire

I am purified
the rain is like holy water

the followers

the roar of Hephaestus's hammering
was utterly drowned out
by the ravaging thunder and rain
the storm building to monstrosity
behind the opalescent house

the smell of green people, green manners
paving the streets and walls of Pleasure Islands
became obliterated by incense
pouring in from the east
behind silken robes of hate

the ripening grain
bowed down before the wind
saffron-robed monks paying homage
to a darkly visaged god
complacent in its carelessness

battle lust was building
the western surf pounding the shores
deaf to all circumstance
but the pull of the moon
and the heat of the sun

the sands of sensibility were eroded
under the powerful pull
of salty nonsense from captives of fortune
prisoners of war
following with bovine senses

not quite living, not quite dying

this isn't how he wanted to die

he'd imagined himself with more wrinkles than caliche
suffocating in a waterless summer

he would keep a well-shoed horse
move to Montana
trail through the peaks
watch the bison eat away at the high school football field
hire the neighbor's boy to shovel the snow

he'd never seen snow

he'd grown up along the Rio Grande
moved east when job prospects dried up

he'd never seen so many trees

even after all these years
he missed the open space
mesquite and horizon as far as a man could see

he felt old

he could feel it in his bones
withered
atrophied so he could hardly walk
not without the possibility of breaking a hip

he could still remember the smell of the horses
hear their snorting and scratching
ready for the fresh hay
brought over from Jacksboro

his daddy's barn

after he'd mucked and fed the pair
he'd brush them one at a time

soft strokes from head to toe
as he whistled absentmindedly
staring at the wormy wood
wondering how the insects died
what they had been searching for
if they'd ever found it

that's how he felt now
pock-marked and bored into
years of faces and needs notching his skin
like a prison wall

being old was like being in prison

on the inside, he still felt such promise
hope
plans for tomorrow
but tomorrow came
and he was still weak
unable to walk out the front door
to drive to the store for food
to ever ride a horse again

the last time he rode a horse
he'd been careless
young foolish
riding the poor animal too hard
too fast

he'd not seen the chasm in the earth
and the horse had stumbled right in
broke his leg

the vet hadn't been able to mend the animal

they'd finally had to shoot him

he now understood what that crippled horse had felt like

only there was no one alive anymore to shoot him
put him down

end the stabbing pain caused by each step of living

there were no more dreams

he no longer slept

slow dance (last stand)

you've survived another night

i watch you
anger boiling against
the rising of the sun
your body's refusal
to surrender to that inevitable
loss

your eyes are
leaden
worn
wishing
for that cold sensation
that arises in the unlit

your lungs expand
contract
in spite of your unwillingness
to allow it

i swallow the salty
sadness
smile slightly
trying to coax morsels
past your objecting lips
but you protest
depositing the undesired bits
on your chin
your chest

tut-tut
i say

as i remove the offense

and reattempt the onslaught
but you stubbornly set your
mouth against my hopes
looking with exhaust
drilling your stare
through shadowed rings
deep into the iris
of my glance

i sigh

i relent

i put the food away
hoping for a better tomorrow
a brighter possibility
that i know will sink with the growing dawn

somewhere
deep underneath the
dark of my diaphragm
i know

i saw your extremities
stained
when i lifted the sheets

i saw the eye of Death
in your upward glance

beach city sunrise

the haze of yesterday's activity hugs the blue horizon
for warmth on this cool and calm winter morning.
tankers dot the landscape like gophers in the
desert, seemingly out of place, but the
waves crash regardless. and the
beach sleeps soundly in its
sandy bed, ignorant of its
troubles or the anger
it should feel
towards
Man.

humble pie

she's in the kitchen again
barefoot
mixing bowl resting in the crook of her arm
the bent elbow holding steady
against the tempest of her whisking hand

she's blending remnants of hope
into the mix of crushed flou(we)rs
the box laying empty on the countertop

she's substituting coupons for miracles
the clippings scattered across the floor

she's out of eggs
and out of time
and her biggest fear
is sour milk
staining her palms
her fingers
when she tries to touch
herself for reassurance

he liked to watch

she was eight. he was only ten.

he liked to watch her
blow bubbles in the air,
soapy shimmer of hope afloat.
they fell on his nose with sweet tenderness.

he liked to watch her
cheering for him in the game
but he was no quarterback,
merely a quad drummer in the band.

he liked to watch her
walking up in white and lace
small, simple, in a dandelion field.
he kissed her with his eyes, hers smiling back.

he liked to watch her
nursing life into their child
the fruit of their affections,
their dreams bundled small, growing large.

he liked to watch her
when she melted in the bath,
toes curling along the tiles
eyes closed to forgotten woes, sinking in the steam.

he liked to watch her
lift out the wrinkles, laughingly,
as she lifted her breasts from weary rest.
he declared every line earned, with joy, sweat, tears.

he likes to watch her
under soil and green growing.
placing lilies ahead, he hopes

she'll be back soon to claim him once more.

he stands close, calling gravely.
now he's the one they're watching.

he's 82. she would have been 80.

saviour (housekeeper of souls)

come into My House
and I can clean your soul

I can sweep your sins
from your heart
if you hand Me the broom

I can mop up the muck
of your past
if you give Me the sponge

I can wipe away the cobwebs
of despair, loss
the mud caked to your shoes
from wandering the wrong path

I will remove the dirt from your life
and hide it on top of the bookcase
in the corner of My living room

when you come later to ask forgiveness
I can empty the dustpan on your head

pathos

Adam's apples

the trees preen
with the slight blush of berries
pink presence among the unripe

rounded
in a taut green
they tempt
merely that tempest of soul
unable to await the summer bloom

frigid
in the winter rush
the hungry shudders
lusty in the piercing tight

the fruit
      falls
   black

fertilizing the infragrant
ground

the feast of sinners

time for a feast
to sate the senses
I the butcher and carver
you the meat on the spit
turning with the force and will
to overpower your strength and guile

you contort in costumed agony
hoping to prey upon the
weak-willed hearts of men

you do not know
the poor and starving
who own nothing
but the meager
threads stretched taut
across their well-oiled backs
hold no conscience against
the art of cannibalism
once the seasoned and well-tenderized meat
is roasting before them

hands do not hear your screams
echoing through the balmy night
stomachs do not see your eyes
melting into the stew
feet do not weep for charred bones
that will one day hold up their houses

as the crackling of the fire
roars high over their heads
noses smell
tongues taste
and all shall be tranquil again
once the spit stops turning

the punishment

he rises
    King Minos
over her landscapes
castigating the form for its excessive
failures. she lies
penitent
awaiting the push
to plant her within
the concentric circles of this
Inferno. he laughs
amorous from her
wary attempt to arouse his wrath.
he ra(i)zes her to her feet
wraps her wrists in binds of leather
and forces her to follow him
through the hallowed chambers.

she whispers softly…

    Lasciate ogne speranza, voi ch'intrate

… and she stumbles
and falls, hair whipping wildly
in a great gush of lusty wind.
the restless torment stirs her blood
to warm her cheeks
and chest, as if his eyes were gouging her
gluttonous, his lips rouging
from a tight-lipped lid of control.
he continues on, dragging her
through the slush of rain, snow and hail
until they face the mad three-headed dog.
he snuffles and slavers at the hem of her
skirts, seeking a wet and warm meal
but Minos holds her secure

heaves a skating blow at the triad of jowls
and leads her on to the great battle ensuing
evermore in that heated valley.

he can tell not the virile
that have lain slain on the battlefield.
their bones have dried
and enriched the canvas beyond scent
or touch. only the inflictions he has caused
remain, thickened in callous. she weeps
at those abandoned in the pitch and mud
stewed by hideous creatures
with giant forks, slobbering mad
over their future meals. but pity dries sudden with fright
at the sight of the sisters
frothing jealous at her blushing.
furies wrapped in snakes, hissing and
slithering in their path
squealing in frissons of terror, mar the innocent's
progression
until great Minos holds aloft a pool
of mirrored obsidian
the oscillating sirens become transfixed by.
and the cession allows him to drag her onward

where she is hauled
infragile goods
through the fiery graves of the epicureans
begging her pleasure
              licking her fingers
                            suckling her toes
dangling
    pregnant
        ripe
          fruit
within grasp of her gleaming teeth.

she falls again
and gasps as Minos raises her high
within his arms, growling bestial
at the slovenly souls over his possession.

   Più non ti dico e più non ti rispondo.

safely held in strong grasp
strong musk of exertion
she is carried across the ochered Phlegethon
into the dark forest of weeping trees.
methodical and meticulous, he unwraps her
binds and straps her to the farthest arbor.

   Here you are, and you shall go no further.

he strips his vestments from his labored limbs
folds them neatly near the captive roots
and falls on her
bodily.
her clothes, already shredded
along the wandering journey by anonymous sinners
give way
complacent, under his unerring hands.

and as he stabs through
inch   by   inch
she shivers, strikes veinal against her binds
and surrenders from exhaustion
falling a third time.

and as he stirs and tears
at the sluices guarding her nethers
the harpies strike her face
her hair
her shoulders

ripping pieces of her flesh from her bones
with every claw and beak that can cut
the bark scraping her arms and exposed back
in withered grooves
lash-like. she cries
hysterical
awash
lost in a shudder of
pain
pleasure
she knows not.
Minos closes his eyes at the sight of her
disfigured
and plunges on, to his own heightened state of sin.

in the final pant, the eternal exertion
the last supper
he causes her to lose the sensation of infliction.
the night tide rises
cleansing, in a sea of ecstasy
and she collapses on the wood
a dampened echo of his removal from her prostrate
form. she realizes her eyes are gouged
but she hears another voice whisper...

Follow me, you know where you ought belong.

she hears Minos acquiesce and shuffle behind
returning to the great whipping storm above
shuddering at the harsh declaration of
Charon
he sputters forth.
she is alone, he tells her
between these bleeding trees
until she can wrap her own rope about her neck.
she is numbed

by the cold air rising from icy Cocytus.
she no longer cares
about the woman-birds biting at her exposed skin.
as her situation settles slowly
into her weary consciousness
she discerns the slight trickle of
blood spuming from the unhealed wounds
sliced vertically above her palms.
she sighs, silently counts the drops, listening
for the uneven splatter upon the dank grounds.
as sound evaporates into the black gape of concentration
she recalls an alternate ending
from a dream lived long ago
before Pandora opened her box
in desperation...

when she whispered softly once...

    E quindi uscimmo a riveder le stele.

demolition

remember our first apartment?
that hole-in-the-wall down on 3rd
where everything was broken
only we never noticed
not initially

remember when we moved in?
it was raining
the first rain in weeks
and we hauled your couch
up the three flights of stairs
only it didn't fit through the door
after an hour of careful angling
incessant shoving and pulling
it fell on my foot
you laughed
as I cursed
hopping about like a fool

even then, you pleasured in my pain

remember when you washed the dishes
and I placed them in the washer to dry
because the damn thing wouldn't clean?
you'd toss soap bubbles at me
I'd throw towels at you
until I had you pinned to the fridge
tasting the skin
of your neck and chest
as you purred like a feline
beneath me
driving me to the brink of madness

remember when you had me
lay those rat traps in our bedroom

after you heard them prowling at night?
funny how the rat it caught was 6'2"
you were on top, writhing naked
in a position you said was for me alone
how you screamed
tried hiding beneath the sheets
we had once shared!
I grabbed my clothes
took your suitcase
left after stabbing a hole through the wall

better than laying my fists on you

now I look up at this building
that housed so much of my pleasure and pain
      (can you really appreciate one without the other?)
as I direct the wrecking ball to fly fast
through the bedroom window once mine
it leaves a bigger hole than I ever could
the cathartic pounding echoing in my ears
I walk over to the concreted debris
only recently released from its abode
grind it to dust under my steel toes

I pretend it's you
with a quiet, private grin

downward from skinned

when you look at me
the molecules
of my being
are disheveled and rearranged
into a frenetic movement
of primordial and philosophic longing

the slight of your stare
the curve of your mouth
distracts me from the cranial crash of
alphabet soup known as language

I falter in the light of your power
the disarming delicatessen of

                                                tug
                                  pull
                        crash
            fall
rise
            swell
                      attack
              retreat

I contract
e x p a n d
swell
and weep
in a small
silent
dry
manner that leaves me
puckering

a parched, shriveled lime
with seeds gaping inwardly

a fig once ripe
frigid with freezer burn
cold and tasteless

for you are the crocus on another lily's leaf
floating on the sea salt roof of the world
far above the valley that consumes me

a   slow   savory   destruction

in violent umbrage

do you hear their ghastly moans
the sound snapping like the flapping
of a canvas flag in the gales that blow
and howl through the sky before a storm?

smell the fight gristling on the soil
the burning fats and stain of sweat
that drizzle and curl up from the ground
the blackened armor that once caged men?

see the ash kicked high by the snarling fire
smoke from the burning floating in the air
like the tatters of grey silk curtains on spectral skin
flung in wraithlike manner against the stilted day?

living in death as they were in life
the inanimate remains lie in broken collage
screaming silently in Picasso's voice
oh, why have you forsaken me?

vindication

on the hard packed earth of the back alleys he stumbles
bare blackened feet shuffling beneath him
a broken ragged washboard without water

eyes he fights to keep on the path straight ahead
leaning lightly on the quiet autos
left to rot along the sidewalk
the only thing waiting for him on the side streets
a bullet and a malicious gaping smile

he dodges a speeding, battle plagued driver
the dust kicking up and scratching at his eyes
but he has not a minute to linger and look

curfew rings like clockwork in the tower
forgetting his surroundings
he dashes for home
pausing at the last turn
he steps with a click of metal
blood dampening the street
from where the trigger has impaled him

in reflex his head turns to the struggle
muffled cry behind him
his own sister
shamed into an unwilling sin against her Maker

without another thought
he misplaces his foot from atop the mine

the Vindication is righteous and sudden

Osama

named by his mother
'Osama, Osama'
the mighty lion that
watches over his herd
protects them from predators
only, he felt small, so scared
in this land of giants.

he was only ten years old...

such a delicate wonder
brought here in swaddling
clinging to his mother's breast.
he knew nothing of the frenzied sand
the land of blood they'd left behind
he was, born and raised
American.
but not to the other kids
the boys chubby in their complacency
pushed impatiently at least
two grades above their intellect.
'Been Laddin, Been Laddin'
they called him
for Osama was his name.

his skin was too dark for them...

he ran to the bus each day
never looking back
for delay, dilly dally
was an invitation to them
their tempers so easy to flare.
soft spoken, dark eyed
his downfall was the day he looked
not down, counting tiles, but up

up at the face of the boy
the one who would be best.
he had to delay a few minutes
at Teacher's request
wondering why he never spoke up in class
when he could always pass the test.

he was only five minutes late...

they surrounded him
cutting off his retreat
taunting him onto the soccer fields
jackals cackling and circling
like vultures around inevitable prey.
they sensed his impending doom
before he even knew
what was going on.
the big kid who had to prove
he wasn't small
the big kid and his lackeys.
the first thing to go
was his armful of books.

he was too small to fight back...

the leader of the pack
knocked off his rimless glasses
and Osama could no longer see
whose fists and feet were flying
towards his face, his knees.
he fought the best he could
but he was half their size
blind and outnumbered.
the shadows attacked from nowhere
and he was left bloodied and barely alive.

he was only ten years old...

there was more of his insides
on the outside, where they didn't belong.
and as the gang continued to kick and beat
the little boy with sneakers and sticks
the big kid couldn't help but feel real pity
real remorse at what they were doing
but speaking up would make him small
smaller than the remains of the boy
who had never caused harm to anyone.
it was just his name
and his skin.

eventually, he declared the game ended.
the boys, pleased with themselves
left for home, kicking trees and
small dogs on the way
anything to make themselves feel bigger.

there is no cure for petty hunger
the desire to inflict pain on the weak.

the leader got home, sat on his bed
looked down at his shoes.
they were so white, so clean
for he hadn't partaken in the
bloody kicking once the boy was down
for the count.
and in stark contrast, his conscience
was oh so dirty, scarred, wounded.

he was only thirteen years old...

he told his mother he wasn't hungry.

what's wrong honey, it's your favorite?
nothing, nothing but his murderous hands.

he sobbed miserably in the privacy of his room
how lucky he had been, born to such luxury.

he attended the funeral
but couldn't bring himself to
look the boy's mother in the eye.

he never played pansy to the pack again.
they called him a pussy, but he didn't care.
he knew what they had all been capable of.

never again would he
crush the weak
the meek
under his hardened feet
guardian of lambs
enemy of giants
named by his mother
'David, David'

candy-colored foes and thoughts of war

I like to segregate my M&Ms
before I devour them

one by one

I pick on the minorities first
after all, they're easier to defeat
and they disappear more quickly
then, I annihilate by color

first Yellow, the least attractive

then Orange, like a disgruntled highlighter
everybody always likes Yellow better!
I'm just as bright I swear I am!

Brown, for being too dark

Green for being too envious of Brown
I wish I was a pretty dark color
not this nauseous glowing hue

Red is history, saucy and defiant
just see if I let you eat me!
I was born for bigger and better things
I belong on top... of a cookie!

and, lastly, my good friend Blue
despite the fact that there are always less of them
they are my last, my favorite
the one child you give the extra kiss too
so the others know who's *really special*

Blue reminds me of the sky
which makes me realize I can't fly
and the chocolate high is suddenly evaporating
into a candy crunch under Chicken Little's feet

I'd better eat Blue first next time
before Yellow starts to suspect something
and teams up with Brown to bring me down

There's nothing so bad as combined forces

just a girl, after all

twelve years
and a virgin of course
but she didn't think much of it

she'd thought
one day
she'd be a woman with many lovers

but now
she's just a girl

a bit frightened
but nothing more

her mother was gone
with her sister
the prized possession
the pretty one
the one that needed protection

he was an odious man

cracked caked fingernails
oily hair flung in a weave about his forehead
yellowed teeth
and a sniggering smile
reeking of rotten meat

she didn't fight though

(after all, he had a knife
and he looked like he enjoyed using it)

best to get it over with

there was a bit of blood
the slightest hint of discomfort
and then it was done

he was done

the police arrived the next morning
(mother had called them, of course)
and they busied bee-d about
comforting the ladies

that the car had not been stolen
that they hadn't been killed

they clung to her convenient lie
like a first-hand smoker
with no more doubt than Mary Magdalene
asleep in the woods
near a cave without a door

(it was none of their business anyways)

it was so easy to believe her
she supposed
for who'd ever want to fuck a fat girl?

child, with child

Daddy said he never wanted no girl
said i's too needy
said i had to go off to da big city
live with *yo big Uncle, got his own bis'ness*

so i leaves ma friends behind,
moves in with Uncle
He drive a flashy car, wear dem fancy suits
but dis house of His ain't much to speak of
peeled plasterin' paint
like sunburnt fleshy flakes
snowflakin' down to da earth
muddy clay dirt, cuz it's alwuz rainin' here
damp and sticky like dried honey.

there's no 'lectricity,
which don't bother me none
cuz ma Uncle says i gotta earn ma keep
if i'm ta eat His food, live under dis roof.
He say da men dat come in to visit with me at night
dey gonna keep food in ma mouth
so who am i to argue?
i do what Daddy and His brotha done say i oughtta do.
i only 'leven years ole, dey know what's best.

ain't long before i start getting sick though.
i wake every mornin'
losin' all i done tried to keep down
da night befo'.
dey's a strange stirrin' in ma belly
i don't know what fo'.

when i mention to Uncle 'bout it
he done threaten to slap me
put me on a bus by the end of da week

give me a letta i gots to give to Daddy
spit on the ground at ma feet
call me *a no good piece of work*
like i bein' lazy
not wantin' to earn ma keep.

i say, *no dat ain't it at all*
but He already got me on ma way back to ma daddy.
i know He ain't gonna like seein' me.

sho' nuff, i gets back home
walks into Daddy's house
He workin up some young thang
like she a shake He gotta mix up by hand.

He take one look at me, say
what you doin' here, you ain't suppos' to be here.

i hand him the letta, tryin' not to cry.
i feels real sick, ma stomach done churnin'
like it's tryin' to make buttuh.
only then, i finds out it's makin' somethin' else entirely.

damn, you pregnant? what you do dat fo'?
I shoulda known you was good fo' nothin'.

i hangs ma head,
lets the tears run down ma face
thinkin' 'bout da child dat's a'growin' inside me.

i hope it ain't a girl.

a promise of peace

every mornin' da creak of da rockin' chair
sounds with da breeze wakin' wi' da risin' sun
that old chair ma daddy made
where I'll never again see ma momma rockin' and hummin'
snappin' them green beans in two

she married young and lived hard
walkin' da mile to da general store every week
carryin' what goods she needed on her wiry back
bent like da reeds along da creek bed
bowin' in a spring breeze
It were'nt 'til I got older that I knew just how heavy flour was
or the burnin' caress of the burlap bag on ma bare neck

I seen her da day she died
like a crumpled paper doll in her daddy's bed
so tiny, so fragile
she looked at me with her woeful blue eyes and said
now don't let dat man o'yo's burn ma chair fuh firewood
ya hear?
and o'course I did.

I's married to dat man 'fore momma was cold in hur grave
he works fuh dem rich folk up in da hills
ev'ry day he go to dem people's ranch
da first colored man dey let step foot on der propertie wi'out
a'pointin dat rifle
he wear his threadbare flannel and sweat-stained straw hat
out der ev'ry day
watchin' dem cows eat 'til da sun is low in da sky
I swear dat hat done look like da floods done rose and
receded on his scaldin' brain
but I sho' do hates it
when he throws ma fryin' pan round and hollas at me
like he done lost his mind

didn't used to be like that
when he was a'courtin' me
he was damn near da nicest man I'd evuh met
beautiful strong hands
soft with dreams dat was dashed to smithereens
on dem rocks out der made o'alabastuh white
the toil done drove him to drinkin'
devil whiskey turn him 'gainst me

but tonite I sits on da back porch
huggin' my heavin' breasts to ma ribs so tight
wi'out a stitch on t'hide me from the blessed moonshine
may it soak up ma pain
and wash away the welts on ma skin
I know he gots a tempuh dat burns hotter dan any star
but da last ting I want is fuh him ta beat me into ash
I luvs him but just cain't take it no mo'!

I prays so hard to ma momma ta tell me what to do
and jus when I gets tired o'waitin' for an answer
well, I don't know if it's da salty tears blurrin' ma eyes
or da red 'n swellin' makin' me see double
but der she is in all her youth and beauty
a dazzlin' apparishun of ma momma
from when I was just crawlin' in da dirt
she say *honey-chile, come wit' me*
and shine in all yo'glorie fuh all to see
you are ma sweet purple butterfly! come along now!

I hears da echo of dem dammed
spurs he likes to wear so much
makes him feel all high and mighty when he's threatenin'
he say he gonna cut me 'cross the neck 'til I bleed
scar my face so no'one'd be recognizin' me

I never befo' felt da rough mud cake o'his boots

and I can smell dat devil whiskey burnin' on da chilly air
but ma momma's here now,
and everythin' gonna be a'ight

da evenin', it's so bright.
she was always so full o'light
ma momma.

she hand me ma quilt, and I ain't cold no mo'.

leaves

the dying leaves blush crimson
and fade to yellow in the falling chilly air.
by winter, their corpses will cover the street.

I walk, the wind curling around me,
coldly through inadequate clothing
until numb with the effort of keeping warm.

the man crumpled on the sidewalk
like forgotten leaves swept to the lamppost,
I step around in trepidation, avoidance.

I do not want to hear the crunch of another soul
beneath my hardened feet, another leaf drifting,
abandoned to brown and crisp in the gutter.

discarded beer can in reach of unstretched limbs
and I wonder if it soaks the knot of cancerous despair
until I hear his guttural groan, a desire for death.

perhaps not.
I walk on, unarmed and unable to face winter.

sixlets

i.

I gave you my smile
inside a heart-shaped box
you used for kindling

ii.

Pandora came at me with a key
stabbed at my eyes
and released my dreams to the wind

iii.

the moon laughs with a gibbous glance
at my pretense of making left turns
when I'm planning to turn around

iv.

there's a door in the desert
the color of sand
that hides an ocean of potentiality

v.

I would dive into the depths of your immensity
but I don't know how to swim
and I'm shackled with the weighty sins of Eve

vi.

how do I show you every atom
the entirety of my cellular makeup
without you cutting my DNA {by walking away}

oil slick

bubble and seep
from fathoms deep
rise liquefied bones and
silenced cries

the moon yanks on that string
connected to the shore
and the sheen blossoms
breaks
and stretches
through the brine
that salty mix of
sweat, skin, scales, and
microorganic thoughts
putrefied by the presence of
rotting algae and dying fish
sinking to the bottom
bellies full of cast stones and
sedimentary eyesight

the light sifts through the surface
refracting with the burgeoning hope
of evolution
so rich that the flavor
is almost distinguishable
against the edge of a
strong summer sea breeze

there is potential here for reclamation
for a cleansing so deep
that the bottom feeders will become visible
from the air, and in the harsh dissection of bright white
they will blink with their cold barren eyes
shiver at the influx of heat
and swim on to deeper waters
where Pandora's folly might be unable to
sleep

eros

ginger crush

when you lick the plump of your lips
I can tell you want to taste me
that slow, salacious stalking
as you slant into my reach.
I savor saliva from your mouth
as you taunt my tongue with yours
running smooth hands along my arms
touch tingling soft on spine.

Tease, I whisper in your ear
gruff and husked with longing.
you kiss me silent, suckle sweet
and linger, loosely, guiling.

reaching hungry 'neath my blouse
you love me lewdly, nip to teeth.
I shudder, ache, with scalding want
fingers comb your curls, approving.

between taut, strictured legs I reach
find your heat brimming, ready.
two fingers reach in depth at first
'til slender fist fills liquid space.

I claim you mine, work meticulous
my darling, as we rock, breast to breast.
and you ease your savagery upon my skin
as I drive you to the brink of bliss

and you tumble over, crumpled, on my chest.

eyes closed, you catch your breath
and I feel you wander to my downy depths
nails prickling along the journey.

orchis dracula vampira

she watches him with orchid eyes
as he rises from his seat
walks silkily behind her resupinate form

tense with unknown certainty
awaiting divination from his aural sects

the grains of the wood feign grit unto her arms
but she blames her siliceous fingertips
for grinding against the lacquered desk

a sign of weakness

she waits

with a loud lemon smack echoing roundly
she hears his palm strike
before the warmth can wander to her cheeks

staggered, the stain of dermal breath
'til tempo rises staccato style

her calyx contracts, blossoms
and he sinks bodily onto her back
hands falling, penitent, beside hers

slowly she intertwines fibrous fingers
a vanilla vine tightly symbiotic

he savors the close-budded clove of her pores
but rises, inching earth-like from her fire
and she closes her eyes, feeling him through the lids

as he recalls the rush of (ex)inhale
as he submits to the Freudian dismissal

and he orders her rapid departure (in)presence
and her tepals fold, wilted in brilliance
and she weeps at the fading of his hand print from purple

to red – the shade of her sorrows colored in sulfites

she needs him to be her savior

if she slices her skin
the aromatic release will rush in a toxic orgasm

she smells cloves and dreams of trees beneath the scars

he will return
his thumb prints remain

incurable

fingers warm
clasping
jugular
clavicle

polished wood
gliding
floating
through oxbow tranquil
trembling below the surface

captain the sternum
wander but not far

altitude causing
the lungs to gasp
shudder
and the peaks to rise stiffly

meander
silently in the hunt
knowing where the prey rests
sipping the cool refreshment
delicate
tense in the knowing of eventuality

lower lies the springs
such a wealth known to few
that you linger
lazily
decadent in the wash of tides
building along your body

a slow collapse as you
inch

into the death pool
smelt into a soft cohesion
languorous as the air bubbles up
from beneath the toes
set free by a violent
rise in temperature

move the mercurial beads together once more

infectious
this euphoria is like a cancer

after b'stilla, before the morning

her hair
infused with chai
spice of hot tea and
honey drops

saffron threaded
'round the bare
of her neck

and the sweat from
heat of night
dripped
dissolved
the delicacy
'til drizzling
down her chest
infusing her skin
with desert marinade

and the drums played
louder
the smoke of bubbled meat
mixing with torching flame
fugitive temptation
from the heavy tajine
buried below

and he placed the remains
of the charmoula on her stomach
and devoured the meal
as slowly as permitted
drinking her sex from her navel
rising in the fall of rapid breath

and the shadows danced

along her length
feisty fairies waving feathered fronds
in the sea-flung wind

and the feast
from the coal-glow
dissolved into shreds of lamb
on her heated tongue
teasingly falling from his
roughened fingers

only softened by the
pumice of her curves
the dark curls
falling over dark eyes
hiding the blush from view

rising from a wandering
caress

and a whispered hush

the almond

I am not like the wild lantana
blooming ostentatiously with color
for every passerby to see

I blossom
behind drawn shades
in the dusken shadows
that caress me in
gilded elongation

beneath
the conservation of clothes
my body remembers
heathen dances
fireside passions
smoldering in
freshly green grass
under tree-limbed sky

the dermis burns
from a desire to be seen
to feel the touch of foreign hands
and teeth
and cheeks

the lower lips
pucker
like the peel of the pistachio
ready to be cracked open
eaten
suckled sweet

once shelled
the sheathing of white almond
glistens

winks with untold secrets
yearning

the bittersweet of cinnamon
the granular sugar
coat the surface like a second skin

it hides beneath this rough layer
waiting for the right mouth to bite through
eyes closed in expectation of
the mixture of textures and tastes
grating softly over the various senses of the tongue.
no flavor will be left unswallowed
as you are wholly transfixed by the
purest hunger
and satiation

but there are so many nuts to choose from
so much waiting to be devoured
the almond smiles through the day
ululations of despair
singing with the moon's marble glow

to be trapped under these scarves of false modesty
when the only want is to be blanched and slivered
consumed and destroyed
replanted and rebirthed
again and again

a timorous potency

let these hands hold the stem
leading to the cup you forage with
bent over bubbling brook
raw with thirsting need.
you shake with every trepid dip
unable to bring the metal to your
mouth

these fingers
feel the strong steely skin
coating a river of enigmatic passions
swirling with the burn of eddies
beneath arterial walls

let them scrape
through the surface
nails marking where you belong
in the geologic scale
gypsum fashioned after quartz

the boiling blue
of your ferric veins
shall break through
flowing up the handle
in red explosion
pooling in my hands
sliding up the skin of my arms
under cheek
around lips
rouged with the life you give
without thought of complaint
because you know no other way
because it is what must happen

and you know I will reciprocate

I taste
at last

you

your mind,
your words
your forged tongue of striking steel

that seeks to dishevel the depths
the blood
sweet and thick
flows smoothly
over parted pearl of teeth
and I lay back
on the imperfect pedicure
of moss and grass
waiting
for you to speak my name
the stones eavesdropping
in false indifference

commune with me

communicate through me with your fingers.
mark length of me with your whorling dermis.
rough turns to soft as affection lingers
the touch of your calm, the wet of your kiss.

show me desire of rouged vermilion
puckered and plumped and ripe for the plucking
suckling sweet before tongue-tied invasion
clasp, halting, ginger nibble to sucking.

overwrought weight of words with savory
spice of skin, ready, warm above shoulder.
natural hedon, you waft unto me
oily smooth upon air threatened smolder.

tease me no more with taunting verboseness.
let me breathe fire from towering closeness.

cocoa flow

he sits there in the corner
right foot resting on left thigh
sipping on another White Russian

watching me

he has secured me
his prize
under a dripping torture device
meant to drive me mad with want

my hands are tied behind me
my legs spread along his field of vision

I struggle
but to no avail

the drops of chocolate fall
onto my shoulders, neck, haphazardly
so as to be unpredictable

the surprise is spine-tingling with every strike of my skin

I shiver with the heat of the melted sweet
the burning blue of his eyes
and the rivulets start to form
the chocolate flow outlining my breasts

my curves

until my toes are detailed in rich dark brown
then he comes to me

he kneels quietly in front of me
as if in prayer

ordering me to watch the ceiling
for he will know if I look

If I disobey
I won't be cleansed

he starts at my feet
the muscle of his tongue
moving up the dripping chocolate lines
slowly   methodically
tracing my form with determined strokes

he doesn't pause at my nipples
but continues up to my neck
nibbling with determination at my earlobe
breathing heavily against the sticky nape
and then he switches sides
begins the downward journey

this time
he follows the curve of chocolate
straight to the depth between my legs

his mouth moves noisily
and I strain fruitlessly against my binds

with his increasing vigor
I can tell that the mix of chocolate, Kahlua, and me
swirling over his tastebuds
has him harder than the maple tree
budding with Spring in front of the house

his hands reach up towards my chest
big hands, strong like a giant's
he kneads and pinches the puckered tips
with an expertise

gained from many years over this very body
the smooth ripples of chocolate
smear and smack under his touch
I am a mess

helpless against his manipulation of me
I am malleable at his touch, soft and rough simultaneously
and at last, I come in waves because he demands it of me
rolling sweet and thick past his lips

disheveled and shaking
finger to toe
I shudder as he rises from his knees
pulls me within his grasp
kisses me with a firm determination
to have me taste my desire
rimmed in chocolate

I suckle his tongue fiercely
seeking more of him
more of me
so preoccupied with the effort
I don't notice his slick entrance
until I'm filled with his growing need
near to bursting

I squeeze in gasps
as he licks more of the chocolate from my skin

his giant hands lingering
at the small of my back
pressing constant for more

the whipping post

do you like it when I leather you
when I ease my gloved fingers along your cheek
down your chest
grazing the patent polish
between your thighs
the plush, pale skin
shuddering sensitive at my touch

softened calfskin
rushes roughly along your length
and your eyes close
mouth thrusting towards the heavens
agape in the gasp of need
your want for more
as you give in to the helplessness
that holds you absolute, before me

I castigate you with languid licks of whip
as you thrash away from, towards my reach
fighting, begging, for the feral heat
wondering if I'll cut your binds
watch you shatter with pained need
as you moan in supplication
for the final release

your feet slide slightly
on the slick stones of the garden
and your knees bend towards me
a necessary surrender that gives you to me
as if I were wielding gravity itself

the ropes cut your wrists
yet the mark won't be permanent
as you struggle to regain your forward position
I step up to you slowly

sure-footed on the smooth rocks

your want strikes me hard on between the legs
and I grab your ass with both hands
violating the strong, supple edges of your mouth
as I ride the squeeze, enticingly without entrance

you spend your passion in dollar bills
and I tumble along soon after
the material of my clothing rubbing your nipples raw
drawing more gnash and groan
as you fight the ties, the desire to rip my corset free

barefoot and amorous

I sprawl licentiously upon the rose-colored chair
one leg propped over the arm
foot dangling deliciously in your direction
head resting mischievous close to my shoulder
sidling a sleepy yet contented smile at you

I am slightly drunk on the amorous affection
you swirl with your tongue beneath your aching lips
as you devour this sight of me
decorum abandoned
ready to be taken

the cotton strap of my shirt
falls in slow motion off my iv'ry shoulder
the other shoe dropping silently
calling you slyly towards my side

you kiss the freckled skin
scratching my neck with the stubble of your cheek

as I moan softly and move deft into your silhouette
you mark my surface in your keeping

mouth on mouth, I now rise to your calling
I draw you in between my knees
ravaging the tender flesh along your uplifted earlobe
as you nuzzle in to my ready chest

teeth graze and flash warmth
as I guide you liquidly to the floor
ready to consecrate the new living room rug

every room of this rambling home begs to be christened
my pooled desire thirsting to be your chalice

# of pain and pleasure

I bind to you with nylon silkened teeth
the leathered skin so tightly 'long my wrist
the gloom like fingers licked does sweet bequeath
a shadowed hide for eyes a'dew in mist

I jolt with sting of wanton on my skin
lick lips 'round rubbered pill shoved firm and deep
I throb for rough and rigid far within
so salt might fall into me, liquid seep

but languish whip unto me now do you
to make desire punish equally
a rose of flourish rises on me soon
and, hard, you grab, spread legs and ass with glee

you wet the tip and rush into me *strong*
with fervent want, I buckle, *come* along

cherry tomato

the dew-laden skin is
taut between my teeth
blush red
as I massage the side with my tongue
teasing the plumpness
with a cautious bite
with an increasing incremental force
until there is a slit in the surface
and then the pillowed seeds
burst forth like a bloom in time-lapse
sequentially exploding in an acidic greeting
the sound echoing like the blast of
an atomic bomb against the inner ear
I continue to taste another
the ripeness wrinkling the surface just enough
to slow down the eruption to the rate of rumbling thunder

the composition slides down my throat
slowly
satisfying with the sweetness of the yin
burning with the ardor of yang

the consumption is complete
the assimilation undetectable to the naked eye
that merely sees us as two disheveled forms
replete

in medias res

run your feathers down slope
where pores pant and pucker
starved for your rigid attention.

slide your taste buds smooth in
'til dripping sweet with salty breath
as I buckle your heart strap tight.

rough your lifelines close to mine
palm out and eyes down, I will
lash your lashes and rouge your cheeks.

suck your whispers, teeth to ossicles
gasp with the splash and crash of secrets
drown me with your muscles, spasm.

drag me from the blackened sand
kiss skin once, then set me free
I lava run 'til you come for me, again.

melagrana salate

cut through the skin haphazardly
to the prize in wait within
dig out the seeds with your fingers
dripping red, then lick them clean

I promise it's worth the stain

rub, tongue 'gainst mouth
wipe the seeds clean
as the sacs of sweet-sour fruit
burst with ripe flavor
in a cool, swimming swirl
of juice that runs down your throat
drippingly viscid to the back

I need no devil to barter me
I've more than six to tempt you

tongue crimson
waiting
tingling with temptation
you spit out white naked seeds
suckle a handful more

I swell with ripening fervor

goddess

goddess
I dance to the beats
you play on your drums
because it pleases me
slow reptilian glide
oiling my skin
against the
very
air
seducing you with the luscious
bounty that lies hidden in my loins
eyes closed, I dream of fire and hot
humid nights, writhing, skin on
skin, alone in this darkness of
incense, hidden amidst each
other beneath long nights
absent of moon, as we
groove in sync, our
sweat dripping
mingling
you worship me, hand
clasping my shivering breast
as it hardens at the tip from the
exertion you set free deep within
my hardened heart that's for this brief
and solitary time yours to manipulate,
caress and suckle with your unceasing
need. give homage to me with every
lunge. slaughter yourself upon my
temple, an offering to the magic
of life that lies in depths below
the curves you long to keep
mistake me not, for I do
indeed belong to
no man and
every man
as well

vibrations

thrust against the wall
fingers of one hand splayed across my neck
the others inside me
viciously, wantonly willing my body to writhe
in painful ecstasy
my throat burns as he licks his fingers clean
and I close my eyes
pretending to be somewhere safe from him
a private haven
but my insides are allowed no weary rest
as he slices me
jams into me like an anchor into the sea bottom
hot tears stream down
as I am moved up and forth against the wall
the bricks
tearing into me like sandpaper claws, and I know
I am bleeding from him
with one final thrust he finishes his task
his degrading smirk
causing bile to swim behind my mouth
and he kisses me
with one last plunge of his tongue
and I taste
the rotten, decaying flesh suckling it raw
as silently
he leaves me there in a wet, discarded lump
shivering
from the haunting memory of echoing vibrations

like bees do

drink from the nectar
pooling
'gainst my glands
before it seeps into the skin
and disperses
like dew on dappled grass

rip out the petals
sweetly
one by one
as they peek out
from the covetous
calyx of my nodes

savor the silky sensation
on the tip of your tongue
as I pollinate your eyes
your chin
that delicate hollow at the base of
your throat

you seek to make honey
as you sting me once more.
the viscous sap hangs low
in a swollen drip
not daring to drop

some like it rough

she grabbed at his belt and pulled him towards her
until their noses were almost touching.

Take these pants off.
I want to see your knees.

he shuddered a sensual sigh and fumbled with the belt button, zipper
never letting go of the contemptuous stare of her eyes.

Scabbed quite nicely, I see.
You've done this before.

with the slightest hint of pleasure, she grinned
wetting her scarlet lips slowly, seductively.
and before he could blink a moment of relief
she had whipped her mark across his back.

Down on your knees, slave.
I won't be asking again.

and he fell to the floor
nearly unable to stop his face long dive
into the wood slat floorboards
covered in only one plush white rug
his sex taut with unspent passion
his hands tied tightly behind his back.
at the sight of it, she growled.

I see you've come out to play.
Down boy, heel, stay.

and, putting down the leather whip, she replaced it
with something much smaller
something rubber with many, many strings.

she squatted, legs apart, in front of him
proceeding to beat him fervently with the rubber whip.

as he squirmed, she cackled merrily
with a full, open-throated laugh.
and he gasped in luxurious pain
unable to draw his gaze from her hands, her legs.

Had enough, have you?
Time for a little mercy?

and she pouted adorably
as she set the smaller device down
grabbing his legs and forcing him on his back.
like a minx, she sauntered over him, purring ever so slightly
removing his boxers as he sprung to life.

My, my, you are a big boy.

her whispered words of tease
before closing her lips around him sweetly.
uncontrollably thrown between rapture and pain
he jutted forward
his pelvis rising to greet her ever so slightly, and she bit him.

he let out a pathetic yell as she leaned back.

Now, now, apparently you haven't been trained properly.
Let's try this once more, I said 'STAY'.

reaching with her right hand
she grabbed her toy once more
proceeding to whip him yet again.
his squeals and pleas falling on deaf ears
through the silky gauze filling his mouth, muffling his cries.

once he was reddened slightly and sobbing gently
she relented
freeing her hands once more.

As this is your first time with me
let's try just the hands, yes?

yes, yes, screamed his eyes, and she giggled
applying a small amount of gel to her hands
she grabbed his sex with her left
pinching the tip, teasing him with her fingernails.

he moaned, writhing slightly
but careful to keep his pelvis on the floor.

Good boy. Now who needs a treat?
Remember don't speak until spoken to.

she kneaded him into a flourish
and just when he'd had nearly enough
she let him go, grabbed the towel, wiping her hands
removed the gauze from his mouth.

Remember, quiet now.
Come have your fill.

and she spread over his face, letting his tongue do its worst.
the burning of her thighs nearly outdone
by the fire within her
until the inevitable explosion
sent her digging her fingernails into his splayed arms.
she shuddered silently
stood over him as he had a good look
and walked over to the leather whip.

Good boy. You learn fast.
Perhaps next time, you'll get a tastier treat.

and smacked him once more with the leather.
his desperate yell of a sob
echoed on the acoustic tiles above.
she laughed once more, wickedly
and walked out the bedroom door
her calves snapping rigidly with every step
her stilettos clacking against the floor in mockery.

he moaned pitifully, lying there, unable to free his hands

or his pent-up emotions.

belonging

buttons fly
Kettle Korn burst
as you roughly remove
the clasp and folds
hiding my sternum from your
undivided attention

other hand
holds my wrists in prayer
beseeching the sky
to collapse in retribution
punishing my flesh
for the wicked of its wet want

waiting for rain to lash me
stinging nettles
of a fine metal whip

in such stormy absence
I melt in the mist
drizzle light on my lashes
as I allow you
to carve your name into my arms
pale, pliant in the weep of night
with the canine of a wolf

tattooed in the ink of your blood
blossoming in rich agony
between dirty clumps of earth
underfoot

unhealing, my arms rest, outstretched
bearing the infliction of unholy stigmata

bruising blueberry crush (reversed)

in the absence of oxygen
you claim from the air surrounding

anything to sustain
your righteous gasp and moan

I suffocate in the richness of wine
as you turn me into water

AsFixia

knotting ropes
'round wrists and ankles

lasso lying languid
'gainst carotid red
waiting to rub skin raw
opposite grasp of gravity

shoving love in
plasticized
to the pooled plethora

ribbing rhythmically pushing
steady heartbeat to rise

hungry lips parting
in symmetric
O

sweat beading on the surface
as exertion forces a cyanic stare

spitting cyanidic pellets
deep throat

reacting with air
turning salt into water
releasing down
the sizzling toxin

and with the mutual mental orgasm

fainting

loss of balance on the whittled stool

hanging

limp and dripping
with wide kohl-eyed vacuity

You will not be cut down
Oxygen will not bloom into your withered cheeks

the noose unravels

you collapse
aground
unmoving

extra credit (after school project)

Teacher smacks the pock-marked desk
barely missing the young hand
holding a nub of a pencil
between fuzzy fingers
thickening in post-pubescence

caressing the slick yellow
painted wooden surface

pink tongue darting out the side
of a hardening mouth

bitten in the surprise
of lost intense concentration.

he pulls the hand towards his chest
cradling, soothing the nearly stinging of proximity
as his tastebuds swell from the growing saltiness
red as white blood cells

he still holds the pencil
thumb moving methodically from the dulled tip
to the curly edge of the shaved wood

the pink prodding of the eraser nub
rubs against his palm
shavings flaking into his lap

lost letters and unrecalled errors
collecting like lint in the corner wall pockets

Teacher sighs
smiles
waltzes like a movie star
back up to her maple lacquered desk

reaches behind the spit-shined red Mackintosh apples
bending so slightly at the hips
to accentuate her seams
(pencils never curved like that)
and returns with a bigger pink eraser

it smells like fresh rubber
and the black letters rub off in his hand
disintegrating condemnation

he sighs
smiles
and removes the curlicues of his name
replaced with block letters

d(wh(y))/d(se(x))

wrap these curves around
the proper axis

(upright)

and discover that integration
over an indefinite
though finite
period of time
will never quantify the mass
of thought
rotating in a continuous
lack of acceleration

the quintic nature of this
reality
leaves your linear mind unable
to comprehend the numerous
irrational solutions
leading to ultimate success

within my sinusoidal development
you strike
haphazardly
at any randomly qualified quantification
but you rise
too quickly
failing to travel even a fraction
of the distance necessary

collapse at a right angle
approach the

(dance)

aligning horizontally with
the tree rings that stretch
smoothly
in each direction.

seek the {} of white
as you are doused
in the sensation
of black {∞}

effice un cibus
ex
illes mens
os
cor
pectus
et
cunnus
de meus

hush

her hands

hovering
the feathered wings
of a cream-colored butterfly

over the sweet of my skin as I slept

afraid of touch
such a thing magnetic
electrically charged as that
that might cause the cilia
on her forearms
to glow

her eyes

illuminating
the slight plump
of her cheek blossoming
like the ripening of a cool peach
on a damp pasture floor
waiting to be
bitten

her mouth

moistened
by the nervous flutter
of her pinked tongue
lingering in the corner in
concentration? consternation? consideration?
wanting to wet the sensitive skin
of my lips
wanting to explore the warm cavern

of my mouth
seeking out its own mate
a bit redder, perhaps
but no less pliant

I shift
and stretch

my eyes

opening
to the sight of her rich brown eyes
confusion clouds, but recognition returns
as I see her hesitate
questions pouring from her
like teardrops

and slowly
she kisses me
as if I might break
into shattered clay pieces
if she pressed too violently against me

then more fiercely
as she forgets herself
and I am awash, tumbling
in the midst of a great flood

her hands

so soft

unlike any man's

like molasses on a soft summer morning

unbuckle straps of shoes binding ankles
unhook garters from your skin, clipped black
roll the stockings down, over scarred knees
palmed lightly as thumbs travel up thighs
to cheeky lace
slipping down, silken

your breath fogging, staggered
as fingers trace nuclear orbits around navel
and wrap around waist, seeking the hooks
binding your breasts
wires underneath falling free as lips graze

your graceful form, curls kissing your neck
tightened throat
teeth punctuating your ripening
until tongue teases in echoing rhythm

rock and sway to upbeats
of a slow Spanish song
violin singing on a high pitch string

tauter than the tight grasp of wet brown hair
under your knuckles
you rise as the tempo slides along faster when the bow

snaps

and you collapse
breathless
eyes closed

heart pounding through the arteries
trembling in your open legs.

a complete permutation

rise now, falling

in jugular anger your passion stands rigid.
cooing, I lick ve(i)nal length with babbling frisson
'til *l'urgences* cause cession to manipulation
as you nuzzle with care my heat, far from tepid.

labial lust burns in mutual starvation
as I grip, tease, untense your soft cranial curls
suscepting stare 'tween thighs, scalding tumult of beryls
and I weep a slight shivered capitulation.

strong you raise on magnificent arms, air razing.
sweet nip and suckle, you resuscitate my moans.
with force of invasion, submit impassioned groans
and shut out close visions of skin, cotton fraying.

in final assertion, capsize on pillowed shore.
still, now, rest steady. on the morn, there will be more.

at the end of her rope

She hung there in the grey-hued, darkened room, the tips of her hair limply brushing the soft beige carpet, her hands gathered at the base of her spine. The ropes only chafed her skin when she fought the binding, so she tried to stay as still as possible. After all, she didn't want down.

She knew this was where she belonged. He had been thoughtful enough to soften the ropes and lotion her skin.

She was grateful to him for the chance to clear her head. The stress of deadlines and client needs had frenzied her into a numbed state. She hadn't even realized it, not until he placed his hand on her back, running his fingers between her shoulder blades. A feeling close to revulsion had crept up her throat.

She'd sworn to herself she would never refuse this man that she loved and trusted with her very soul. The fires of any human-made Hell were nothing compared to the burning in his eyes.

She had failed to submit. This was her punishment.

Now, the blood was rushing to her head, making her light-headed. She might have fainted. The sensational pain was close to the warmth of ecstasy when she dreamed of him, his hands, hands of a multitude driving her mad with want.

Undulating with the pulsing of her own imagination, she hadn't heard him coming towards her. But there they were, two pale, hairy calves invading her line of sight, the muscles flexing as he shifted his weight from one leg to another.

"How are you doing, Mara?"

"I will do your bidding." *And whomever else*, she added silently.

"Of course you will. And you will beg, or should I say *moan*, for more, slave."

"Yes, Master." And she meant it. She needed to know for herself if she could feel, really *feel*, again. She was glad he wasn't touching her yet. She liked the solitude.

Lost in her thoughts once more, she didn't realize he had bent over until she heard his voice, felt his hot breath right next to her ear.

"Know this, my sweet siren. By tomorrow morning, you won't be able to walk."

As he rose up straight, her spine snapped in a slight fear and tinge of excitement. *But he wouldn't really hurt her.* On cue, the ropes dug into her thighs, the skin where her buttocks met her legs, reminding her of just what a predicament she really was in. Mara prayed briefly for something nameless. She wasn't sure what just yet. But she knew somehow that Michael did.

For what seemed like interminable hours, he left her there, looking at the inverse image of these familiar walls. Perhaps she drifted in and out of sleep, she couldn't really tell. But the tranquility from her helplessness calmed her, allowing an almost meditative state. Letting her mind wander, she began to recall thoughts she had long ago forgotten; fantasies, fears, causes she had once felt so passionate about. Mara had let herself grow complacent in so many different aspects of her life. She had let herself die, or at least the person she had thought she was.

Hot tears began to pour out of her, streaming down her red curls and soaking into the carpet. They were followed quickly by heaving, silent sobs that rocketed through her entire body, only tightening the knots holding her there.

But crying would solve nothing. Slowly, Mara worked to slow her breathing, blink her reddened eyes free of the last few drops clinging to her lashes. She then twisted her head as much as possible, blowing air back through her nose, trying to expel as much of the self-pity as she could before Michael returned. She had just managed to slow her pulse, breathing, when she heard the doors banging his arrival. Luckily, she could explain away the flush in her cheeks through gravity.

She heard Michael's muffled voice then purposeful steps until the bedroom door opened. He was once again standing in front of her, she staring at the dark blue wash of his jeans.

She reached out to caress the rough material with her cheek. He stepped back out of reach before she could.

"Slave, you will not touch me until I say you can. You do not deserve to lick the concrete dust off my boots. Not yet. You owe your penance."

Michael's words rained down upon her in a steady, clear voice, yet intimate in timbre. He must have practiced this speech. She knew if she said, 'stop', he would. But she wasn't ready to leave this package unopened. And she knew better than to speak. *A slave never speaks.*

"I want you to know what your punishment will be, that you might think long and hard on it, be prepared, and not try some pathetic attempt to use your feminine wiles on me as method of escape. I want that vivid imagination of yours to humble you into complete submission."

Mara hung on his every word, like cold honey dripping from a string. She was hooked. If she'd been upright, she probably would have collapsed to the ground, her inner thighs wet with unspent desire.

"I have hired a couple of day workers for my use. They don't speak much English, so don't worry about conversation. I'm going to watch them core you out until I know you're good and punished. And don't worry, you'll be blindfolded."

He reached down and placed a smaller rubber ball in her mouth as a gag, binding it in place before blindfolding her. As he walked behind her, the full impact of his words finally sunk in, her eyes widening behind the dark material.

He was going to allow some stranger to have her! *Two strangers*, she quickly reminded herself. Mara's stream of thoughts and visions was violently interrupted when she felt his fingers covered in cold liquid, probing her anus dutifully. He almost knocked her breath from her body when he inserted a plug forcefully into her.

"There, that should get you good and ready."

And with that he left her alone again, hanging there. She almost started sobbing again, in frustration. She wanted to pummel Michael, twist on the tip of his penis and nipples with her fingernails in retribution! But of course, she would never have had the audacity. She was helpless, besides.

Then, the images of her penance began to play like a reel in her overactive mind. Maybe this was what she wanted all along. *Maybe...*

Absentmindedly, she began wiggling her ass around in the air. The plug was huge, nearly painful, and she felt her body trying to remove it. But she knew it was there for a reason. Concentrating on the slow sound of her breathing and the rapid pounding of her pulse, trying to fight her body's impulses, she didn't notice the door had opened until she heard Michael's voice, his sweet words that she used to love so. Tonight, they were steel.

"There she is. Have at her. Here is a box of condoms and lube. You'll need it. She'll be bone dry from the inversion."

Mara knew he was speaking more for her benefit than theirs. And she heard their eager groans, the unzip of metal on metal, the ripping open of condom wrappers, the squirting of lube on their rigid and ready members.

She felt the first come up behind her, his large and calloused hands running along her taut legs, up to the ropes, loosening them slightly to lower her into a better position. Her head was now nearly touching the floor. Mara then felt him squeeze her buttocks in his palms, one hand removing the plug with a deft movement. She puckered in relief, until he began playing with his fingers, applying extra lubrication at the surface. Then the sheathed tip pushed slightly into her. She shuddered as he eased his way in, feeling him tremble from his own excitement. He kept coming in until she felt his balls grazing the top of her butt cheeks.

And then he proceeded to pound into her, shaking her whole body, legs shuddering, breasts flopping in perky virginity. It seemed like an eternity, but this man didn't have the standing power to resist the tight force of her buttocks. Soon, she felt him come with a final heaving shudder that seemed to have no end, lifting her slightly from the floor.

No sooner had he finished with her then she felt the second man greedily shoving his way into her. She thanked Michael silently for the excessive use of lubrication, knowing otherwise she would be red, raw, and wounded from this incessant pounding. This second man lasted somewhat longer than the first, trying to play a bit with her exposed clit until a harsh word from Michael, *I said no playing*, had his hands back around her glistening waist. He managed to lift her further from the floor, evacuating her anus with a slow lingering slide. He kissed her inner thigh and left her there.

Deaf with desire, Mara failed to hear Michael's voice, the closing of zippers, the shuffling of satisfied men until the blood in her body sank slowly from the skin, cooling slightly below boiling.

She was trembling, her breasts ached, her entire body shivered in gaping need, ready to be filled. Where was her Michael?

Mara heard him return a short time later. When he entered the room, she fought against her bindings, moaning around the gag he had placed earlier in her mouth.

"Be still."

At his voice, Mara calmed her limbs, willing them to be still, for him, for Michael. He reached down and removed the gag, leaving the blindfold in place. She worked her tongue and jaw back and forth, relieved at the departure. Mara then felt Michael heaving on the ropes as she swayed slightly, he lifting her farther from floor than before.

She heard the sounds of discarded material, and when he removed her blindfold, she was looking at his naked form.

Her head was right at the level of his crotch, a one eyed beast staring straight back at her. She rubbed her tongue against the back of her teeth with desire.

"Take it. It's yours."

As he stepped towards her, she opened her mouth, willing his swollen member between her lips as far as she could. She suckled the tip, running her tongue along the length, lavishing her longing along every inch he would give her. Mara felt, in return, his tongue, his soft kisses running along her thighs, along her navel, until delving into the warm skin hooding her clit. As she sucked, he sucked, and they bucked into each other with a rising tumult of unspoken emotions, breathless passions.

He came in a wrenching spurt of salty semen, and she swallowed him with the determination of satisfaction she wanted to be his, his alone, so richly deserved, so long in the coming. As she licked her lips seductively, he backed away, slowly, staggeringly, grabbing his shirt from the floor.

"I'll let you down in the morning, slave. You did well."

Joy and disappointment combined in a bitter battle for supremacy over her heart. An excitement she hadn't felt in years began to pour over her, dousing her more thoroughly than the sweat dripping over her face and through her hair ever could. As she floated on the cusp of consciousness, lost fantasies began to curl and lick at her imagination, like rising incense. She closed her eyes, wetting her lips, concentrating on the flourish of images, feeling the tingling excitement spread along her skin like goose bumps.

Mara let herself hang limply, lost in the sensation of her tongue running along his chest, as it writhed in her mouth in mimicry. She heard the drip of water in the bathroom sink, the sound of Michael tossed amid the soft cotton sheets they usually shared. The intoxication of longing left her boiled down to her animal instincts. If there had been a moon in view, she was sure she would have howled in return.

Tomorrow morning, she would release this spirit that had devoured her, taken over her throbbing limbs, boiled heart. And Michael would surf the waves with her. She might not be able to walk tomorrow, but she would definitely ride. She would master him with servitude.

Acknowledgements

Some of these poems have previously appeared in collaborative works from NeoPoiesis Press, the Poetic Pinup Revue, and ETC: A Review of General Semantics.

Excerpts from Rumi have been included with permission from Coleman Barks.

About the Author

Erin Badough is a licensed professional engineer who currently resides in San Antonio, Texas, with her French Bulldog. She has a Bachelor's and Master's degree in Environmental Engineering from Texas Tech University and enjoys writing, drinking red wine, cooking real food, volunteering in her community, and traveling to other countries in her spare time.

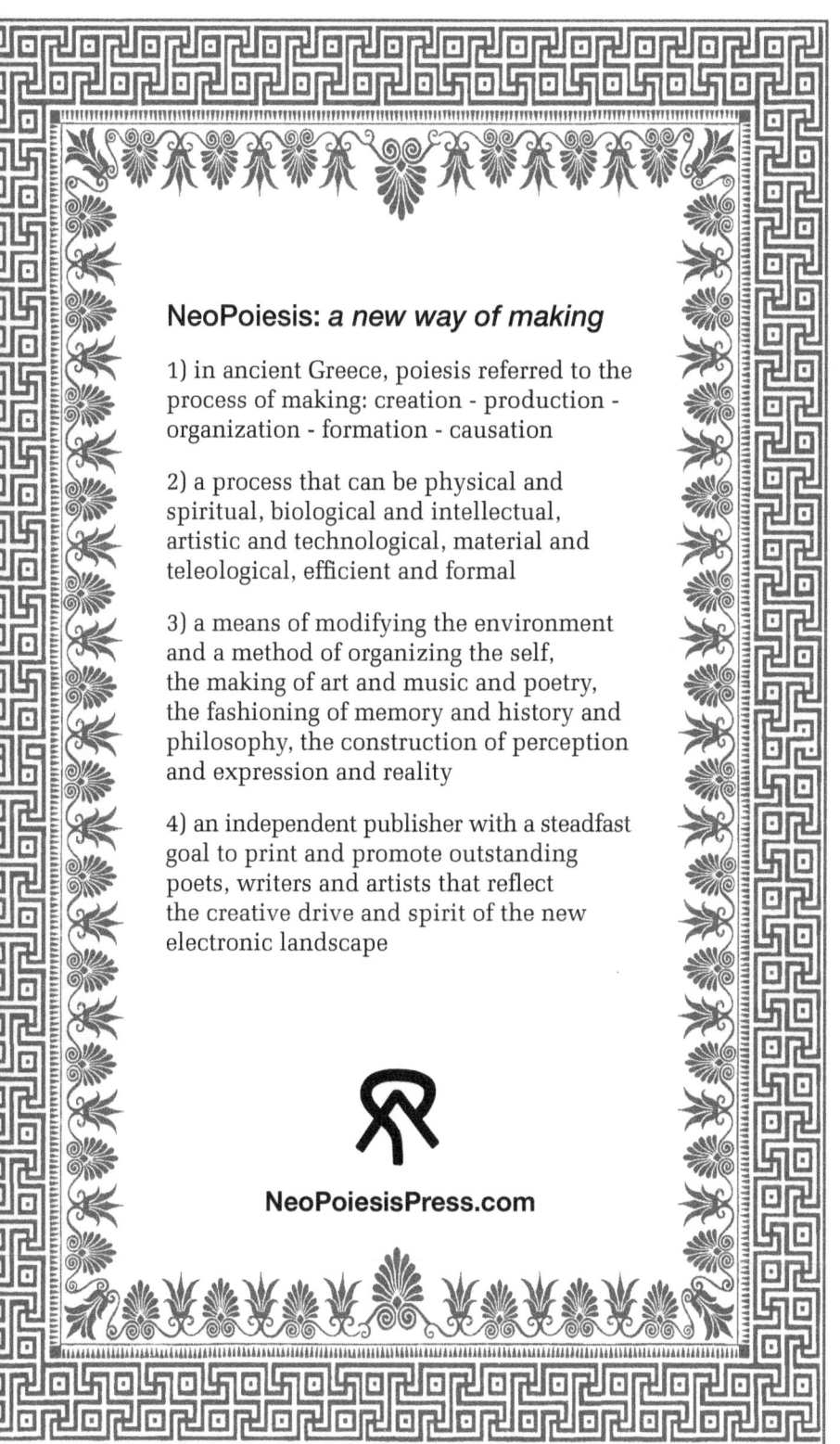

www.ingramcontent.com/pod-product-compliance
Lightning Source LLC
Chambersburg PA
CBHW021004090426
42738CB00007B/643